FastStart

Your Business

Everything You Need to Know About
Starting Your Sole Proprietorship

Ronika Khanna CPA, CA, CFA

CONTENTS

TO THE READER

Complimentary PDF Version with Links

Throughout this book there are links to various resources that do not appear in the print version. If you would like a complimentary version of the PDF with links, please email me at ronika@montrealfinancial.ca along with proof of purchase, and I would be happy to send it to you.

Reviews and Feedback

If you find this book useful, I would greatly appreciate a testimonial or review on the website where you purchased it.

Alternatively, if you think the book doesn't address certain issues or you are left with lingering questions, I would very much like to hear about that as well.

You can leave your comments directly on my website by completing my feedback form or send me an email at ronika@montrealfinancial.ca.

INTRODUCTION

When I was first starting my own business, I spent a great deal of time scouring every available resource for information on what needed to be done. This was a long and tedious process, and I often wished there was a resource that would give me comprehensive guidance on the process. One of the problems was that, while I had an idea of some of the procedures, there were others where I didn't know what I didn't know and was therefore not even able to pose some of the questions.

Over the past 10 years, as an accountant and a business owner, I have amassed a trove of information on what every new business owner should know. This has allowed me to advise numerous business owners in a variety of different industries on how to set up their businesses. And while each business has its own set of unique goals and challenges, the procedures for setting up a sole proprietorship are similar across all businesses.

I have created this guide to consolidate the information that I wished I had when I was starting my business. I want to simplify the process of starting your business so, once you have followed the steps and answered the important questions, you can dive right into the exciting parts of building your business.

WHAT IS A SOLE PROPRIETORSHIP?

According to Canada Revenue Agency (CRA), the definition of a sole proprietorship is as follows:

A sole proprietorship is an unincorporated business that is owned by one individual. It is the simplest kind of business structure. The owner of a sole proprietorship has sole responsibility for making decisions, receives all the profits, claims all losses, and does not have separate legal status from the business. If you are a sole proprietor, you also assume all the risks of the business. The risks extend even to your personal property and assets.

How Do You Know if You Have a Sole Proprietorship?

The simple answer is that if you are selling any type of product or service, on an ongoing basis, and you are not employed by another organization where you receive an employment income slip such as a T4, you essentially have a business. If this business in not incorporated or part of a partnership with one or more individuals, then you are a sole proprietorship.

Examples of Sole Proprietorships

There are various types of businesses that operate as sole proprietorships, such as:

- If you sell web design or photography services in your spare time
- If you sell goods on eBay on Etsy etc, on an ongoing basis
- If you have a website that makes money from ads

- If you have a website that makes money from affiliates
- If you are a writer with one or more publications
- If you sell your services on Upwork or Fiver or similar sites
- If you receive donations as an individual for your work
- If you are a driver for Uber or other ride sharing services

What Are the Responsibilities of Sole Proprietors?

Sole proprietors might have to register their businesses in the province in which they are located. This is usually dependent on provincial regulations and is discussed in depth in the next chapter.

Any business that earns income and is not incorporated is required to report its income on the T2125 form, on an annual basis, which forms part of the personal tax return.

All businesses that have sales exceeding $30,000 must register for sales taxes. There are some exceptions to this rule, which is discussed in detail in the sales tax chapter.

Businesses may deduct reasonable expenses from the income that they earn. Many businesses have expenses that are common, such as rent, office expenses, telephone and internet expenses, and hosting for your website etc. Other expenses might be specific to the business type.

For example:

- Fees that you pay to Uber or other ride sharing services
- Publishing costs for your book
- Photography equipment
- Commissions paid to intermediary sites such as Ebay, Etsy, or Fiverr for listing your goods or services
- Cost of raw materials to make your product

A comprehensive discussion of expenses can be found in the chapter on expenses.

Business that claim expenses should maintain copies of all receipts, bills, invoices, and other source documents.

What Are the Advantages of a Sole Proprietorship?

It is usually very straightforward to set up a sole proprietorship. If you use your first and last name, you are usually not even required to register and can start operating as a business right away. If you decide that would like to have a name that isn't your full name for your business, then provincial registration is quite straightforward.

The accounting and tax reporting is usually fairly simple and, in many cases, can be done by the business owner.

If your business loses money, this can be used to reduce your income from other sources and the corresponding taxes payable on your personal tax return.

What Are the Disadvantages of a Sole Proprietorship?

Since there is no legal separation between the owner and the sole proprietorship, the business owner is responsible for all the debts of the business. If you decide to stop running your business tomorrow, you are still responsible to pay any amounts owing to suppliers, the government, banks etc. In extreme cases, this can potentially put all your personal assets at risk, including your home and investments. This is different from a corporation where the liability is usually limited to the assets of the corporation and does not extend to the business owner.

A sole proprietorship might seem less professional than a corporation and as such might have difficulty getting contracts, bank loans, or even sub-contracts.

All profits from an unincorporated business are added to your personal income, which in turn raises your tax rates. There is no flexibility as to when you can declare profits. They are taxed in the year in which they are earned.

An unincorporated business does not benefit from the small business capital gains exemption, which means that if you sell your business you would have to report the sale price (less expenses) on your personal tax return as a capital gain. Conversely, a business owner who sells a corporation that qualifies as a small business is exempt from capital gains of approximately $400,000.

Starting a business in Canada is remarkably easy. You mostly need to have a marketable product or service and be aware of certain obligations. Once you are armed with knowledge, you can go ahead and start your business!

WHY AND HOW TO REGISTER YOUR SOLE PROPRIETORSHIP

Should You Register Your Business?

Once you have decided to start a new business and have concluded that the best structure for your business is a Sole Proprietorship, the next step is to determine if you need to register it. If you are using your exact first and last name, and only your exact first and last name, then you are not required to register your business, regardless of which province you are located in. However, if you are using a business name that is anything other than your own name, you are required to register your business, except in Newfoundland and Labrador.

Note that a Sole Proprietorship does not have legal existence in the same way as a Corporation. It is simply a name that is used to represent your business to the public. Consequently, Sole Proprietorships do not have limited liability, and the owner/operator is responsible for the debts of the business. For all practical purposes, the you and your business are the same entity.

How Do You Register Your Business?

Note that this these instructions only address business name registration requirements for unincorporated sole proprietorships in each province. In addition to registration, you should also consider whether you need to register for sales tax (HST/GST and QST or PST). Additionally, all sole proprietorship owner, regardless of size and whether they are registered, must report their business income or losses on their personal tax returns.

Alberta Registration of a Sole Proprietorship

1. Choose your business name

The name doesn't have to be unique; however, you cannot use the words limited, incorporated, or corporation (or any abbreviations thereof).

2. Get business name report (optional)

A NUANS member can provide you with a report that details names, trademarks etc. that are similar to your proposed name. This step is not required. The cost of a NUANs report is approximately $50.

3. Complete the application for a trade name

Download or print the PDF from the website (step 3) and complete the application. The information required includes:

- Trade Name
- Type of Business
- Location in Alberta
- Date on which the business begins
- Name/address of the applicant
- Statement/Signature

The form, which is editable, can be completed using any PDF software.

4. Submit your Application

Unfortunately, in Alberta the application cannot be submitted online. Instead, the form must be taken to an approved service provider/business registry along with:

- The application
- ID
- Applicable fees
- NUANs report if completed

The fees for registering an Alberta sole proprietorship are relatively nominal at around $50. Since there are numerous service providers, and the service is relatively straightforward, you can generally find a reasonable price.

British Columbia Registration of a Sole Proprietorship

1. Choose your business name

The name must be unique; in addition, you cannot use the words limited, incorporated, or corporation (or any abbreviations thereof).

2. Apply for a Business Name

Unlike Alberta, you first have to apply for a business name in BC. The will verify the availability and validity of your name. This can be done online, in person at Service BC, or by mail by completing the Name Approval Request form and mailing it in.

The fees to apply for a business name are $30.

Once your application has been approved you will receive an "NR (name request) number". You must use this NR number within 56 days or risk having to reapply for a new name request.

3. Register your Business

The business registration can be done online at "OneStop". You will need to create an account, enter the information requested and pay a fee of $40 (in addition to the $30 for name request). You can also download, complete and mail this application along with the requisite fee. The registration approval process usually takes about 2 days.

Manitoba Registration of a Sole Proprietorship

1. **Choose your business name**

The name must be unique; in addition, you cannot use the words limited, incorporated, or corporation (or any abbreviations thereof).

2. **Reserve your Business Name**

File a name reservation with the Companies Office. This can be done online by creating an account with the Companies Office or by downloading the application and mailing it in along with the fee. The cost for reserving your business name in Manitoba is $45. There are specific guidelines for choosing a name in Manitoba that should be reviewed since, if your name is rejected, you will have to reapply and pay an additional fee.

3. **Register your Business Name**

Register the sole proprietorship by using the business name registration service either online with the Companies Office or download, complete, and mail the form along with the fee. The fee for registering your business name in Manitoba is $60.

New Brunswick Registration of a Sole Proprietorship

1. **Choose your business name**

The name must be unique; in addition, you cannot use the words limited, incorporated, or corporation (or any abbreviations thereof).

2. **Get business name report**

Once you have selected a name for your business, you must obtain a name search report from a private-sector name search firm. This report must be an Atlantic-based NUANS search report. A Google search will provide a number of organizations that provide this service. The cost is approximately $60.

3. **Send the Registration Application**

You may register by mail using Form 5, Certificate of Business Name. The fee to file for a New Brunswick business registration is $112.

Alternatively, you may file online by using the SNB online service This must be accompanied by an electronic copy of your NUANS (Name Search) report along with the covering letter from the name search firm. The NUANS report must have been done within the last 90 days and set out the proposed name of your business. The application should be accompanied by your email address or shipping address and fee of $112.

Newfoundland and Labrador Registration of a Sole Proprietorship

If your Sole Proprietorship is In Newfoundland and Labrador, there is no provincial government registration required.

Nova Scotia Registration of a Sole Proprietorship

1. **Choose your business name**

The name must be unique; in addition, you cannot use the words limited, incorporated, or corporation (or any abbreviations thereof).

2. **Reserve a name for your business**

Before registering your business, the Registry of Joint Stock Companies needs to approve the name. There are guidelines on choosing a name, which can be found here. The fees for reserving a name are $61.05. The application for the Nova Scotia name reservation, which can be downloaded in PDF format, can be sent via mail. It can also be completed online.

3. **Register your Business**

Once your name reservation has been approved by the Registry of Joint Stock Companies then you can go ahead and register. The fees for registering your business are $68.55. Payment must be included with your application. If you meet all the requirements, the Registry of Joint Stock Companies will issue a Certificate of Registration and Business Number. It should take 1 to 2 weeks to get the Certificate of Registration and Business Number. It can take longer if more information is needed or if your application wasn't filled in correctly.

Ontario Registration of a Sole Proprietorship

1. **Choose your business name**

The name must be unique; in addition, you cannot use the words limited, incorporated, or corporation (or any abbreviations thereof).

2. **Get business name report** (optional)

You can use the Enhanced Business Name Search which is available at Integrated Business Services Application. This step is not mandatory. The fees range between $8 and 26 for a name search.

3. **Register your Business**

In Ontario the reservation of the business name and the registration of the business is combined into one application. You can complete the registration form online. The fees for registration of the sole proprietorship in Ontario are $60.

You may also download and complete the PDF and mail it or drop it off to:

> Ministry of Government and Consumer Services
> Central Production and Verification Services Branch
> 375 University Avenue, 2nd floor
> Toronto, ON M5G 2M2

The fees for sending the Ontario business registration application by mail or in person are higher than online at $80 per application. Once the application has been submitted, you can expect to receive your "Master Business License" within 20 days.

Prince Edward Island Registration of a Sole Proprietorship

1. Choose your business name

The name must be unique; in addition, however, you cannot use the words limited, incorporated, or corporation (or any abbreviations thereof).

2. Apply for approval of the proposed name and name reservation

If you intend to register a business name in Prince Edward Island, you must first submit a name approval request to reserve the proposed name. Reserving a name requires you to complete the name approval request in the Online Corporate and Business Names Registry. This reserves the name for you but does not approve it for use.

Submit the non-refundable payment to search and reserve the name. Payments must be made online when submitting your name reservation. The fees to register a sole proprietorship in PEI is $90.00. The Registry Office will review your name (typically, within 5 business days). You will receive an email if the name is approved. Registry Office staff will call or email if they have any questions. If the name is not approved you will receive an email with information on how to contact the Registry Office.

3. Apply for business registration

The application may be processed online at the new online business/corporate registry. Once you have set up an account you would choose the application to register a business.

Quebec Registration of a Sole Proprietorship

1. Choose your business name

The name must be unique; in addition, you cannot use the words limited, incorporated, or corporation (or any abbreviations thereof).

It is critical in Quebec, even if your business name is English, that you provide a French version of the name. This French name is considered the primary name in Quebec, regardless of the business owner's desires. You must ensure that the name of Quebec business conforms to certain requirements which can be found in this related article.

2. Register the name and business

Similar to Ontario, the reservation of the name and registration of the business are completed in one step. You may do so online. The service is only offered in French; however, can use Google translate to help with any comprehension issues.

A business that must register must do so within 60 days of starting operations. The fees to register a sole proprietorship in Quebec are $36.

Once you have completed the form, Registraires des Entreprises will review your application, including the suitability of the name that you have chosen for your business. If you they accept your application, they will provide you with an NEQ number which is the official number of your business. If they reject your application, they will let you know by mail, and you will have to resubmit.

Saskatchewan Registration of a Sole Proprietorship

1. **Choose your business name**

The name must be unique; in addition, you cannot use the words limited, incorporated, or corporation (or any abbreviations thereof).

2. Reserve a name for your business

Log in to the Corporate Registry application. Once you have created an account, select "Business Names" and select the "Reserve Name" option. Then, in the "Reserve for" option, select the purpose "Saskatchewan Business Name Registration", another drop-down menu will display, entitled "Type"; select "Sole Proprietor" and click "Continue".

You would then enter in your proposed name and click on "Check Name". The system will tell you if similar or exact names have been found or if the name is available. You will also need to enter the nature of your business. Fees for reservation of a Business Name in a Saskatchewan entity are $50.00.

If your request is approved, you will be sent a name reservation number. Note that the name reservation number is required to register your business. This name registration is available for 90 days after approval.

3. Register your Business

When you fully complete your name reservation and you are issued a name reservation number, you can then submit your registration through the same online registries portal, by clicking on "Register".

Fees for registration of Registration of a Business Name are $60 + GST.

Depending on your province, the process of registration can be as simple as completing an online form and submitting a fee. Other provinces have a two-step process; however, in most cases the process is usually fairly quick. If you are using a business name other than your given name, it is important that your register as soon as possible after you start your business to ensure that don't face any issues with various provincial regulatory authorities.

WHY YOU SHOULD SET UP A SEPARATE BANK ACCOUNT AND CREDIT CARD FOR YOUR BUSINESS

Once you have registered your business, the next step should be to set up a separate bank account. This is a simple and effective measure that allows you evaluate the financial performance of your business.

Why You Should Have a Separate Bank Account for Your Business

- **Stay Organized**

Setting up a separate bank account when you start your business is one of the easiest tools available to organize your finances. For those of us who procrastinate and leave administrative tasks such as accounting to the end of the year or even closer to tax time, a bank account that is solely used for business transactions can be invaluable in assessing where you stand with respect to your finances at any given time. By referring to the balance in your bank account, you have a good idea of how much cash flow you have to spend on your business and how much you have available to pay yourself. Although unincorporated business owners do not technically pay themselves a salary for tax purposes (they are taxed on the total profit earned from the business - amounts withdrawn to pay yourself are not considered expenses), it is a good way to discipline yourself as you can limit how much you withdraw to a fixed monthly amount, while any excess funds are used to develop your business.

- **Separate Business from Personal**

Another important to reason to have a separate bank account for your small business is to ensure the separation of business from personal transactions. In the event of an audit of your small business, the revenue agencies are likely to ask for your bank statements. Providing them with statements that combine personal and business banking will at a minimum lead to probing questions about non-business-related deposits and expenses. At worst, this could result in them assessing you on amounts received that are not business income, or they could disallow expenses. It is then up to you to object and contest the assessment, which is about as pleasant as getting a root canal. A separate bank account avoids this potential problem.

- **Avoid Manual Data Entry**

Online accounting software like Quickbooks Online and Xero allow you to download your banking transactions automatically, which helps to reduce manual data entry of transactions and also ensures that all business related transactions are captured.

- **Conveniently Pay Business Taxes**

A separate business bank account allows you to conveniently pay business taxes using online banking including sales tax, payroll taxes, and corporate income tax.

- **Capture All Business Transactions**

Having a dedicated bank account that is reconciled on a regular basis (i.e. all entries on the bank statement are matched to your accounting records) ensures that you properly claim your expense deductions and ensures that you don't understate your invoices.

What Are the Limitations of a Separate Bank Account?

- **It's Not an Accounting System**

A bank account, while helpful for understanding cash flow, does not replace an accounting system that would provide you with information on how much your customers owe you or how much you owe your suppliers.

- **Does not Provide Info on Outstanding Transactions**

While the bank balance at the end of the period might give you some indication of profitability, it is far from exact. Additionally, it does not give you information on cheques that you have issued but have not yet been cashed nor on deposits that may have been received but not yet processed.

- **Additional Fees**

A frequent objection that I hear are fees that banks charge on business accounts, which can be high depending on the type of account that you have. On the plus side, these expenses are deductible from business income.

Why You Should Also Have a Separate Credit Card for Your Business

- **Separate Business from Personal**

A separate credit for your business can also be invaluable in helping to separate business from personal finances. It can also prevent personal transactions from showing up in your business accounting.

- **Don't Forget Business Deductions:**

Many business owners tend to forget business expenses that are made on mixed use credit cards resulting in loss of business expense deductions (the net result of which is higher taxes!).

- **Payments from Business Bank Account**

Payments of your credit card balance should be made directly from your business bank account which gives you an even better separation of business vs personal and a more accurate picture of cash flow.

> ➢ *Note: A credit card does not have to be a business credit card as long as it is a separate credit card that is used mostly, preferably entirely, for business.*

Other Considerations

- **Discipline**

For this system to work, it is important to be disciplined in using the bank account and credit card that have been designated as much as possible for business transactions. If you are unincorporated, you would transfer a certain amount on a regular basis to your non-business (personal) bank account. As mentioned above, ideally this amount represents a regular "salary" rather than ad hoc transfers whenever you require funds.

- **Personal Is OK**

Also, if you are not incorporated, the business bank account does not necessarily have to be a formal "business" account (which usually carry higher fees) but can just be a separate "personal" account. The downside of not having a separate "business" account is that you won't be able to use it to make online tax payments. Similarly, your credit card can just be another "personal" credit card that you use solely for business. It is important to note that if you are a registered business with a name different from your own, then you will have to set up a separate business bank account to receive payments, particularly in the form of cheques made out to your business name.

- **It's Easier, Overall**

While have a proper accounting infrastructure is important for every business owner, no matter how small, it can be difficult for the self-employed to have time to take care of all aspects of their business given limited time and resources. The simple step of setting up a separate bank account and credit card for business purposes is a significant tool to help small business owners maintain better control over their finances without having to do much additional work.

SHOULD YOU REGISTER FOR SALES TAX AND WHAT IT MEANS TO BE ZERO-RATED?

When starting your business, it is essential to consider whether you are required to register for the Goods and Services Tax (GST) and Quebec Sales Tax (QST), or the Harmonized Sales Tax (HST) in appropriate jurisdictions. The simple answer is that if you anticipate that your annual gross revenues (total sales) are going to exceed $30,000 and your products and/or services do not qualify as Zero-Rated or Exempt, then you are required to register for GST &QST / HST. Zero-Rated or Exempt businesses are those that provide products or services on which sales taxes do not apply and are explained below.

Taxi operator or commercial ride-sharing driver

If you are a self-employed taxi driver or commercial ride-sharing driver (which refers to services such as Uber and Lyft), you must register for the HST/GST regardless of your revenues. This effectively means that you have to register on the day that you start operating your business. Generally speaking, Uber will both automatically register you for GST and QST in Quebec and collect and remit the amounts due on your behalf. You just have to prepare the HST/GST and QST return at the end of the year.

Should You Register Even if You Expect Less than $30,000 in Annual Sales?

Even if you do not meet the threshold of $30,000 for mandatory registration or if you are providing exempt or zero-rated goods or services, it might still make sense to register. Consider the following:

Reasons to Register for HST/GST and QST Even if Your Sales Are Less than $30,000

- The primary benefit of registering for sales tax is that it allows your business to claim back 100% of HST/GST and QST that you have paid on business-related expenses. This is particularly helpful to startups and businesses that have high up-front costs such as computers and equipment as well as rent, office expenses, travel etc. Many such businesses have no sales in the beginning and the recovery of sales taxes can help reduce costs significantly.

- Not being registered for sales can communicate to your clients that you are small and by extension might imply a lack of professionalism and/or experience.

- Since customers/clients expect to pay sales taxes anyway, it is rarely a deal breaker. Also, if your customers are primarily businesses, it has no real impact on their bottom line as they are able to claim back their businesses related sales taxes as well.

Reasons to Not Register for HST/GST and QST if Your Sales Are Less than $30,000

- For those that have started a side or hobby business such as selling goods on ebay or providing web development services in their spare time and who don't expect their businesses to reach $30,000 in sales, at least for the foreseeable future, you might not want to take on the administrative burden of registering for sales.

- If you are primarily providing goods or services to individuals or businesses who are not themselves registered for HST/GST, it may be a competitive advantage if you do not register for and thus do not charge HST/GST, since your price will be lower compared to businesses who are registered for sales tax.

- Business owners/self-employed workers who want to do as little administration as possible and not have to worry about tracking sales taxes and potentially paying penalties and interest for late filings.

- This often applies if you are still in the startup stage and not sure about the viability of your business idea.

What Does It Mean to Be Zero-Rated or Exempt?

Products and services on which you are not required to charge HST/GST and QST are referred to as zero-rated. Included in this category are prescription drugs, groceries that are not for immediate consumption, and exports outside of Canada including services provided to US and international customers. Small business and self-employed individuals whose goods or services have been designated as zero-rated, can still register for HST/GST and QST (see above) as they are allowed to claim the Input Tax Credits (i.e. sales taxes paid for supplies and expenses). For example, if you provide services to clients internationally (e.g. the United States), you are not required to charge HST/GST and QST in most cases; however, you may still claim back any HST/GST and QST paid on business expenses. This can be a substantial benefit for businesses and freelancers. See links below to see list of zero-rated supplies:

- Canada Revenue Agency (CRA) Zero-Rated Supplies and Services
- Revenu Québec (RQ) Zero-Rated Supplies and Services

How Is Zero-Rated Different from Exempt?

Zero-rated goods and services allow businesses to claim sales taxes paid on expenses while goods and services that are exempt mean that businesses cannot claim sales taxes on expenses paid. For example, doctors provide services that are exempt and may not claim taxes paid on their rent and other expenses. As such, many of them don't even register for sales tax.

- CRA Exempt Supplies and Services

Deciding whether to register for HST/GST and QST is a determination that should be made based both on the tax requirements as well as business considerations. If you do not decide to register right away, you can always do so in the future. However, keep in mind that you might lose the ability to claim tax paid on expenses previous to your registration date, which can add up, particularly for businesses that have high start-up costs.

HOW TO REGISTER FOR HST/GST AND/OR QST

How to register depends on whether you are located in Quebec or elsewhere in Canada. If your business is located in Quebec, administration of both GST and QST is done by Revenu Québec. However, if you are located anywhere else in Canada the administration of HST/GST is done by Revenue Canada. If you are located anywhere else in Canada and also have business in Quebec, you would register with CRA for HST/GST and then register separately for QST in Quebec using the methods described below for Quebec (except you would only register for QST).

> ➤ *Note: The process for registering a sole proprietorship, partnership, or corporation for sales taxes is all essentially the same.*
> ➤ *If you are changing your business from a sole proprietorship to a corporation, you MUST register a new business corporation and apply for new HST/GST and QST numbers if applicable.*

If Your Business Is Located in Quebec

> ➢ *Note: For businesses that are registered in Quebec both the GST (which is Federal) and the QST are administered by Revenu Québec.*

You can register for GST and QST in one of four ways:

1. ONLINE: By using the *Register a New Business* service (to register for sales taxes, payroll source deductions, and corporation income tax).

2. ONLINE: By accessing *My Account for Businesses*, if you are already registered for clicSÉQUR with Revenu Québec (you can access the service in the Consumption Taxes section in My Account).

3. PHONE: By calling Revenu Québec's client services.

4. MAIL: By filing form LM-1-V: Application for Registration. Revenu Québec - Registering for the GST and QST.

If Your Business Is Located Anywhere Else in Canada

You may register for HST/GST in one of three ways:

1. ONLINE: By accessing the CRA application.

2. PHONE: By calling 1-800-959-5525. Before calling this number, review the form in part 3 below to make sure that you have the necessary information.

3. MAIL OR FAX: By mail or by fax by completing the RC1 form and supplying the information for the business accounts that you need.

SHOULD YOU OPT FOR THE QUICK METHOD OF REPORTING HST/GST & QST?

If you are self-employed or a small business with annual sales between $30,000 and $400,000, it might make sense to select the Quick Method of reporting your HST/GST and QST, which is essentially a simplified method of reporting sales taxes . While regular reporting of sales taxes requires that you calculate all amounts collected and paid on eligible expenses, the quick method (or simplified method as it is also referred to) requires the application of a single reduced rate to your sales while HST/GST and QST paid on expenses is not deductible. The key details of the Quick Method and its suitability for your business are discussed below.

What Are the Eligibility Criteria to Use the Quick Method?

For HST/GST purposes, annual taxable sales must be less than $400,000. QST requires that annual taxable sales be less than $418,952.

There are exceptions to businesses that are permitted to use the Quick Method. The following types of business **cannot** use the Quick Method:

- Accountants/Auditors/Tax Consultants
- Financial Consultants
- Lawyers
- Municipalities, Colleges and Universities, and Charities.

What Are the Rates Used for the Quick Method?

GST and QST

If 40% or more of your sales are from goods that were purchased for resale (e.g. all objects or things that may be perceived by the senses and are movable at the time of supply: a vehicle, animals, furniture, etc.):

- GST Rate = 1.8%
- QST Rate = 3.4%

If your cost of goods sold is less than 40% (effectively, you are a service-based business):

- GST rate is 3.6%
- QST rate is 6.6%

For both GST and QST purposes, you are eligible for a 1% credit on your first $30,000 of sales when using the Quick Method.

HST

HST Quick Method Rates depend on the province.

> ➢ *Note: The Quick method does not affect the actual rate of GST and QST that is charged to customers and clients, which are 5% and 9.975% respectively.*

When to Use the Quick Method

Since the Quick Method is simpler than the regular method of reporting HST/GST and QST, it can be a great way to fulfill your tax reporting obligations while simplifying your accounting system.

The Quick Method of remitting GST can result in a significant savings; however, this is largely dependent on how much GST you pay on purchases (also known as Input Tax Credits). For example, a service-based business that uses the quick method rate of 3.6% and has $50,000 in taxable sales and $5,000 in taxable purchases would save $660, which can add up over time.

Since the quick method implicitly reflects Input Tax Credits (sales taxes paid on expenses) i.e. by reducing the rate that has to be remitted to CRA or RQ, no separate calculation for expenses is required (nor allowed). As such, taxes cannot be claimed on purchases/expenses except with respect to sales taxes paid on capital purchases like a car, computer, or real property, which are claimable. A capital item represents a purchase that has a useful life exceeding one year and usually exceeds $400.

However, a business that has higher costs in the beginning such as a startup might actually be paying more by using the Quick Method as their purchases exceed the threshold by which the Quick Method results in net savings. It is extremely important to make this determination before electing to use it. On the other hand, if you only have a small number of expenses, like many service-based businesses such as consultants, programmers, and contractors, it can make a lot of sense to use the Quick Method.

How to Register for the Quick Method

To use the Quick Method in Quebec ,you must complete form FP-2074-V, Election Respecting the Quick Method of Accounting for Small Businesses, and file it with Revenu Québec. Acceptance of the election will be confirmed in writing.

To start using the Quick Method for HST/GST anywhere in Canada , except Quebec, you must complete election form GST74 Election and Revocation of an Election to use the Quick Method of Accounting. The application can also be made using CRA's My Business Account.

The deadlines for the application for the Quick Method are as follows:

- For Quarterly or Monthly returns, it must be before the due date of the filing. For example, if you file quarterly and your due date is April 30th for the period from January 1st to March 31st, the election must be filed by April 30th.

- For Annual returns, it must be no later than the first day of the second quarter. This would be April 1st for all businesses with a year end of December 31st. For any other year end date that is not the calendar year, the due date for the election is three months + 1 day after the year end.

> ➢ *Note: Once the election has been approved, it can be revoked after waiting for a minimum of one year.*

SHOULD YOU DO YOUR OWN SMALL BUSINESS ACCOUNTING?

When starting your business, it is easy to be overwhelmed by the number of tasks you have to learn, one of which is accounting. While many business owners can cobble together a sense of their financial situation through (as a former boss used to say)" back of the envelope" calculations and reviewing their bank balances, there is still a need for an accounting system that can validate your calculations and provide you with data to ensure that your business is going in the right direction.

Setting up an accounting system can, however, be intimidating for many business owners. Accounting can be technical and requires an understanding of certain terminology to be most effective. Prior to technology, business owners would either have to outsource their accounting or hire personnel to take care of various entries and ledgers and consolidations. These days, however, there is a number of software and apps that can significantly simplify the process and allow any business owner that has a genuine interest in understanding their own data to do the accounting themselves. Answering the following questions can help you determine whether it makes sense to do it yourself:

1. Are you a new(ish) business?

Probably the best time to set up your own accounting is when you are a startup or new(ish) business owner. This is because you likely don't have that many transactions and you might have some time on your hands while building up your business. Additionally, your requirements are much simpler in the early stages than when your business starts to become more established and consequently more complicated.

2. Do you have a separate bank and credit card for your business?

One piece of advice that I give most business owners that are just starting up is to set up a separate bank account and credit card that are used mostly for business. There are many advantages to a separate business bank account, one of which is that accounting software such as Quickbooks, Xero and, Wave accounting all allow you to download your transactions directly, thereby reducing massive amounts of time (and tedium) on data entry.

3. How many transactions do you have a month?

If you expect your startup to only have a small number of transactions, it makes sense to do your own accounting as these can be fairly easy to track with the right accounting software.

4. Do you prepare your own invoices for your clients?

If you send invoices to customers/clients yourself, then setting up an accounting system right from the outset makes a lot of sense as this is a significant part of the work. All accounting software has the functionality to create and send invoices (many of them also have time tracking). With most software, you can email invoices to your customers from within the software and some even allow you to collect customer payments by clicking a link on the invoice. (This requires an initial setup with the software but once done can be a fairly seamless process). Payments collected directly are then posted and reconciled automatically, saving time.

5. Do you want real time data?

For some businesses, having access to real time data can significantly benefit their operations. For example, if you sell handbags, you might need to track exactly what you have in stock at any given time and ideally you can depend on an accounting system to give you this information. If your operations are still relatively small, and you are already entering your own invoices, it is fairly easy to enter the other transactions to ensure you are up to date.

6. Do you need to assess your cash flow regularly?

Some businesses need to know exactly where they stand with respect to their cash flow at any given time. Review of your bank balance gives you a sense of this; however, it does not tell you how much you owe to vendors or how much you are owed from customers. Additionally, you might have loans or interest payments that are coming due or you might have other purchasing commitments that have to be met. If this is the case, you might want to consider doing your own accounting until your business is big enough to outsource or hire a bookkeeper.

7. Are you comfortable with technology?

Having some experience with general purpose software and/or cloud based apps is an important consideration when evaluating whether you should do your own accounting. If you haven't used technology much, the learning curve for a new accounting software will be steeper and as such will require a bigger time commitment.

8. Do you like numbers especially as they pertain to your business?

Do you have a sense of excitement when you see how your business is doing? Do you enjoy seeing how all the numbers come together and looking at your profit and loss? When you see your numbers, are you interested in deeper analysis, customer behaviour, what products or services are most popular, etc.? If so, doing your own accounting helps you be closer to your numbers, as you have a better understanding of the flow from original transaction to the final report e.g. when you enter an invoice, it shows up a sale on your profit and loss report.

9. Do you have an accountant or an accounting resource that is accessible for questions?

Since most business owners are not accountants, there are some technical transactions and treatments that can be difficult to wrap your head around. The day-to-day of entering your transactions can be fairly straightforward, but it helps to have a resource to whom you can turn when you are not sure how to do something, as this can help with you avoid mistakes that many small businesses make that can take some time to undo or, worse, result in incorrect reporting and potential penalties.

10. Are you comfortable doing your own tax reporting?

Businesses have various tax obligations that are dependent on structure e.g. sole proprietorship vs corporation, employees/payroll obligations sales tax registration status, etc. Some of the tax reporting is fairly straightforward and can be done by the business owner with a little bit of guidance. However, as your startup grows in size, these obligations can become increasingly complex. As such it might make sense to do your own accounting while outsourcing your tax obligations to an accountant.

In the past, doing your own accounting was time consuming and usually not worth the burden on the business owner's limited amount of time, which could be spent more valuably elsewhere. However, cloud-based accounting software has changed all of that as it has significantly reduced the amount of time and knowledge required to do your own accounting. There are also numerous online courses and trainings available to help business owners navigate their accounting, making something that used to be quite inaccessible much easier to navigate.

HOW TO SET UP YOUR ACCOUNTING

As discussed in the previous chapter, setting up your own accounting can be fairly straightforward, particularly if done as part of starting your business. There are three main options:

Use a Spreadsheet

If your business has a minimal number of transactions, you are not incorporated, and you don't expect it to grow much in the future, it might make most sense to use a spreadsheet to track your revenues and expenses. Both revenues and expenses should minimally have the following information:

- Date of transaction
- Name of customer (for sales) and supplier (for expenses)
- Category for expenses e.g. office expenses, rent, direct purchases
- Amount before sales tax
- HST/GST
- QST (if applicable)
- Amount after sales tax
- Description of expense

Use Accounting Software

If you have just started your business and do expect it to grow over time, or if you have more than a few transactions a month, I highly recommend using accounting software at the beginning to save yourself the hassle of moving everything from a spreadsheet . It also saves time, as accounting software have many features that automate routine tasks. My recommendations for accounting software for most new business is either Quickbooks Online or Xero, both of which are fairly straightforward to use, have numerous online resources for learning and for which monthly costs are fairly low. Both of these software have a large ecosystem of apps that can be used as your business becomes bigger rather than having to switch to another software.

Outsource to an Accountant

A third option is to have an accountant take care of your books. While this makes sense if you don't want the hassle of doing your accounting yourself, the downside is that you don't have the visibility and control if you were to do it yourself as discussed in the section above. The cost is also usually higher.

HOW TO INVOICE YOUR CUSTOMERS/CLIENTS

While it is good practice to register your business and determine the type of accounting system you are going to use, you can usually go ahead and invoice your first customer even if you haven't done these things yet. However, it is essential to determine if you are required to register for sales taxes as this will determine your final invoice amount.

How to Prepare an Invoice

Invoicing can be done in the following ways:

1. By using a word processing software or even a spreadsheet. A template can be set up that can then be saved as a PDF file and emailed or printed mailed to your customers.

2. Accounting software is recommended when you have more than a few invoices a month as it can result in significant efficiencies and allows you to review your history by customer, product, or service, etc. (reporting options are endless). You can set up one or several templates in accounting software, upload your logo, set up sales tax codes to apply automatically to specific customers, etc.

3. Invoicing apps are particularly convenient when you are visiting clients, as with tradespeople or home-based services. These allow you to generate an invoice on the spot and also accept payment using a credit card processor such as Square or Quickbooks payments.

4. Handwritten receipts (although these are becoming less common since most people have a smartphone or technology at their disposal)

Information to Put on an Invoice:

An invoice can have some or all of the following fields:

- Name of customer
- Date of invoice
- Invoice number
- Address of customer
- Your company name and/or logo
- Your contact details
- Type of product/service being provided
- Rate and Quantity or Total Amount
- Description of products or services
- HST/GST number issued by CRA (usually ends with RT0001)
- QST number issued by RQ (usually ends with TQ0001)
- HST/GST amount and/or QST amount
- Total including sales taxes
- Payment details e.g. wire transfer or e-transfer info

Sales Tax and Invoicing

If you are registered for sales tax, it is mandatory to put your sales tax numbers on the invoice. If you are doing it using a spreadsheet, you can usually put them either under the customer contact info or in the main body of the invoice (or anywhere you like as long as they are on the invoice).

HST and GST rates are usually based on the location of the customer. For example if you are a Quebec-based company that provides web development services to customers in Ontario, you would charge them HST at the rate charged in Ontario, which is 13%. Similarly, if you were invoicing a customer in British Columbia, you would charge them GST only, which is 5%.

There are several provinces that have Provincial Sales Tax (PST) in addition to GST. It is important to note that you are only required to charge GST or HST to customers in other provinces. Since PST is not part of the Federal HST/GST regime, it only applies if you have a presence or certain amount of sales in that province.

QST is a bit more complicated as it is actually part of the HST/GST regime, but is not usually required to be collected by sellers outside of Quebec UNLESS they have more than $30,000 of sales in Quebec.

If your customer is outside of Canada, you are not required to charge HST/GST or QST. However, you should make yourself aware of any international sales taxes that might apply in your situation.

> *Note: As with all matters relating to tax, the rules relating to sales tax can be much more complicated. The rules described above apply to typical and straightforward situations.*

HOW TO CALCULATE CPP CONTRIBUTIONS IF YOU ARE SELF-EMPLOYED

What Is CPP?

The Canada Pension Plan is a retirement plan for all Canadian workers that earn employment or self-employment income. Every year you are required to contribute a percentage of your salary or **active** income, based on a fixed rate up to an annual maximum. This results in a pension amount that everyone who has contributed to will receive in proportion to the amount contributed, which you can start taking as early as when you are 60 years old. The standard age that people start taking their pension is usually 65. which can be extended to age 70. The amount you will receive is based on a complex calculation that is affected by the following:

- the number of years that you have contributed to the pension plan
- your average earnings over the time period that you have been contributing
- the age at which you start taking your pension

To qualify you only need to have made one contribution, although the benefits in this case would be minimal.

The maximum amount of monthly CPP benefits is $1,175.83 in 2020, if you start taking your pension at age 65. This amount increases or decreases depending on whether you decide it to start taking it before or after the age of 65.

> ➤ *Notes:*
>
> ⇨ *If you move provinces from Quebec to another part of Canada, you are still entitled to the full amount of pension and would apply for CPP benefits as these are automatically transferred when you move. The same is true if you move from Canada to Quebec, except you would apply for QPP benefits.*
>
> ⇨ *If you move out of Canada to another country, and have contributed to the CPP or QPP, you are also still entitled to benefits even though you are no longer living in Canada.*

How Do CPP Contributions Apply to the Self-Employed?

As an employee, your employer takes on the responsibility for paying certain payroll deductions to the government, which are deducted directly from the employees' gross salary. The net salary, which is the amount on the employees' paycheque, is the amount received after payroll and income taxes have been deducted. Included in payroll deductions are amounts payable to the Canada Pension Plan (CPP). With respect to CPP, in addition to being deducted from the employee's paycheque, the employer is also required to remit an equal amount to the government, which is basically a cost to the employer for having employees.

While employees who receive a salary only contribute the employee portion of CPP as explained above, when you are an unincorporated small business owner that reports income on a T2125, you are essentially taking on the roles of both employer and employee. Consequently, self-employed individuals are required to remit both the employer and the employee portions of the CPP to Revenue Canada. The CPP is calculated annually based on your taxable self-employment income. If you are using tax software to complete your personal tax return, it will be automatically calculated and reflected in the balance owing. The actual remittance to Revenue Canada is calculated based on your self-employment income for the calendar year on your tax return and is remitted through your payment of year-end taxes. 50% of the total contribution is a tax deduction on your T1.

What Is the CPP Contribution Calculation for Self-Employed Workers?

Contributions to CPP can be a significant portion of taxes payable at the end of the year. As such, it is beneficial to know the amount that might be due based on your estimated self-employment income so that you can plan for your tax bill in advance. The 2020 CPP rate for the self-employed is 10.5%. The maximum amount of earnings on which CPP is applicable is $58,700. This means that, if you earn more that $58,700 from your business, then no CPP will apply to income over that threshold. It should also be noted that there is a deduction of $3,500, which means that anyone who earns less than $3,500 does not have to contribute.

To calculate your CPP contributions, you can use our CPP calculator.

While contributions to the CPP can seem like a significant amount, note that you are contributing to a pension fund that you will receive back when you reach retirement age.

WHAT TYPE OF EXPENSES ARE DEDUCTIBLE?

Generally, any expenses that are incurred to earn business income are considered to be deductible. Expenses are deducted from sales to calculate the net profit for your business. Since income tax is based on profit, it is desirable to deduct as many expenses as possible in order to reduce taxes payable. One piece of advice that I give all of my clients is to ensure that the expenses that they are deducting are reasonable, specifically when it relates to "soft" expenses such meals and entertainment, travel, home office, and travel. An unusually high expense in a specific category can be a red flag for CRA and RQ.

Types of Business Expenses

- Direct costs of running your business
- Wages, Salaries, and Benefits paid to employees
- Amounts paid to subcontractors
- Rent, utilities, insurance, property taxes, and other office space costs
- Office supplies/services and equipment
- Information Technology Equipment/Services
- Software/Service Subscriptions
- Telephone expenses
- Conference expenses including travel
- Transportation costs
- Advertising expenses
- Professional dues such as those paid by doctors, lawyers, accountants etc.
- Accounting, legal, and business consulting fees

- Bank charges and interest on loans, including credit cards
- Credit card fees incurred on payments received from customers
- Meals with a business stakeholder such as a customer, supplier, accountant, subcontractor etc.
- Life insurance premiums (Only applicable where the beneficiary is the business)
- Capital Assets (i.e. larger ticket items $400+) including Computer Hardware
- Automobile expenses
- Home Office expenses
- Uniforms and Clothing expenses

Other Considerations for Business Expenses

- **Tax Software:** Sole proprietorships and unincorporated businesses are required to include their business income and expenses in their personal tax returns by completing the T-2125. This form can be found in all online tax filing software including Ufile and TurboTax.

- **Hobby Business:** Care should be taken to ensure that the business is not regarded as a hobby, otherwise tax deductions/expenses that exceed the income of the business will not be allowed.

- **Accrual Method:** Business are required to record their revenues and expenses based on the accrual method. This means that both revenues and expenses are based on the date of the invoice/bill rather than when payment is received or made.

- **Keep All Receipts!** It is extremely important to keep all receipts, bills, invoices, cancelled cheques, and deposit slips. If you have any doubts, then keep it! Also, ensure that you retain all documents received from the government, including assessments and notices. A good practice with respect to business documentation is to scan it (or save electronic copies) in an accounting folder on your computer along with a backup. You may then dispose of any physical copies as long as you have a clear and legible electronic copy.

- **Business Loss Limits:** Excluding CCA and home office expenses, losses can be used to reduce income from other sources and corresponding income taxes if you have an unincorporated business. Corporations are separate entities and as such losses cannot be deducted against personal sources of income. Sustained losses over a few years will, however, lead the CRA to look more closely at your business. As such it is important for business owners to take care that there is a reasonable expectation of profit.

WHEN ARE THE TAX FILING DEADLINES?

The income tax filing deadline for sole proprietorships in Canada is June 15th, compared with April 30th for individuals. However, it is important to note that taxes payable are due on April 30th, after which any amounts due start to accrue interest. Penalties will apply if the tax return is not filed by June 15th.

For sole proprietorships who are registered for HST/GST and QST, have less than $1.5 million in sales and have selected an annual reporting period, the deadline for filing their GST-QST returns is April 30th. Penalties, particularly from Revenu Québec can be significant, so it is important to file and pay these by the deadline.

Some businesses also have quarterly or monthly sales tax filings. It is very important to be clear on your filing periods to avoid penalties and interest, which can be severe.

Tax instalments are required for individuals that estimate they will owe in excess of $3,000 and are due March 15th, June 15th, September 15th, and December 15th. Both CRA and RQ will inform individuals if they owe instalments, the amounts due, and the due dates. If instalments are not paid, the revenue agency will charge interest starting from the due date of the instalment, at a rate that is currently about 5% annualized.

Sales tax instalments are also due for businesses that owe over $3,000 in GST and/or $3,000 in QST. The government usually does not notify you about the amounts, so you have to have to calculate this based on the previous year's amount payable. If you owe quarterly instalments, you would remit 25% of the GST and QST owed in the previous year on April 30th, July 31st, October 31st, and January 31st.

HOW MUCH SHOULD YOU PUT ASIDE FOR TAXES?

Many business owners become so involved in running their businesses and the day to day operations that they forget that they will have taxes to pay at the end of the year. How much tax you will pay will depend on how much profit (revenues minus expenses) you earn in your business. It is very important to take other sources of income into consideration to estimate your final taxes payable. While this is different for everyone, I have found this tax calculator to be very useful in determining how much you will owe in taxes at the end of the year.

Once you have determined your taxes payable by using the tool above (or one of the many others available on the internet), you should put these funds, aside ideally in an interest-paying savings accounts.

Similarly, HST/GST and QST collected from customers should also be put aside in a tax savings account to ensure that you don't spend it. While ensuring that you have the funds to pay both income tax and GST/QST is very important, if you are in a position where you have to choose to pay one , it should be the sales tax. This is because the penalties for non-payment are steep and the consequences can be significant. Bank accounts can be frozen for non-payment, which is a situation that should be avoided if at all possible.

HOW TO PAY YOURSELF AND YOUR EMPLOYEES

Since sole proprietorships are taxed on the profits of their business on the business owners' personal tax returns, the amounts that the owners withdraw from the business are irrelevant from a tax perspective. In other words, you may withdraw any amount of funds, whenever you want from your unincorporated business. From a business perspective, I often advise my clients to pay themselves as if they were employees of the business, as this can give them a better sense of their performance and encourage fiscal discipline. You might decide to pay yourself a fixed amount every month. Any funds that are left in the business can then be used for business growth or savings.

There might however come a time when you decide that you need to hire employees. This is usually an excellent sign as it means (a) the business is growing and (b) the small business owner has learned to delegate. It also means that additional paperwork needs to be filled out and additional taxes need to be paid. The simplest option when deciding to augment your workforce is to have the new worker invoice the business as a contractor, based on hours worked or some other formula. Unfortunately, there are very specific rules as to who qualifies as a self-employed contractor. Essentially, if your worker is working full time, has little flexibility in the schedule of work, and you provide the tools, then the tax authorities will classify them as an employee. In this case, you must take your new worker on as an employee, register for payroll, pay them a salary, and submit regular, periodic payroll reports and payments to the Canada Revenue Agency (CRA). As usual, if you live in Quebec, you must submit to Revenu Québec (RQ) as well. The registration procedure is discussed below.

How Do You Register for a Federal Payroll Account?

Whether your business is a sole proprietorship, a partnership, or a corporation, you will first have to ensure that you have a Business Number. The options below allow you also register for a Payroll Number:

- ONLINE: Register for a Business Number and payroll number online using this link. This will take you through an interview process where you submit the requested information. If you already have a Business Number, you would provide this and complete the payroll section.

> ➢ *Note: The online option is probably the fastest way to have your application processed.*

- PHONE: Register by calling 1-800-959-5525.
- MAIL: Register by completing the Request for a Business Number form and mailing it to your tax center. This form also allows you to register for payroll at the same time, which is included in Part C. If you already have a Business Number, you would complete the payroll deductions form where you must include your Business Number, your business activity, and other information per the form above. Similar to registering online, the form requires you to indicate how many employees you intend to have over the next 12 months, how often you will pay them, and to answer a few other questions relating to the business itself. If you are not

sure, you can use your best estimate. There is no penalty for changing the number of employees or estimated revenues etc.

How Do You Register for a Quebec Payroll Account?

If you operate a business in Quebec, you are required to register both Federally (see above) and in Quebec. Similar to the Federal registration there are three options for registering a payroll number with Revenu Québec:

- ONLINE: If you already have a Business Number, you should register for a *clicSÉQUR My Business Account* with Revenu Québec. Once you have completed your registration, log in to *My Account for Businesses* where you can then apply for a payroll account directly. in the "Source Deductions and Contributions" section.

- PHONE: You can also call Revenu Québec to register for your payroll number.

- MAIL OR FAX: The application for registration, form LM-1-V will need to be filled out for the sections that you are applying which would "deductions at source" in this case. You can also apply for a Business Number at the same time, if you haven't already done so. Note that you will need to enter your Quebec Enterprise Number (NEQ) and your Business Number obtained from the CRA. The LM-1-V allows the business to get a Quebec identification number which is required for all tax files.

How Do You Pay Monthly Remittances (Deductions at Source) to Revenue Canada?

Once you have registered for a payroll account with CRA, you are ready to go ahead and make remittances. Note that employers must register for a payroll account before the "first remittance due date". The remittance due date is on the 15th of the month following the month in which you first pay your employee. Thus, if you issue paycheques to your employees in August, the payroll remittance (Deductions at Source filings) are due by September 15th unless you have received a notice allowing you to file quarterly or annually. This information is also usually available in CRA My Business Account.

Amounts to be deducted from employee paycheques and remitted to the CRA include Employment Insurance (EI), Canada Pension Plan (CPP), and Federal Income Taxes. There is also an employer contribution component of EI and CPP.

There are several options for setting up your payroll, paying employees, and calculating deductions at source. If you choose to submit the remittances to CRA yourself rather than outsourcing it to a third party, you have a few options.

- ONLINE (using Business Banking): Most Canadian banks (RBC, TD, CIBC, BMO, etc.) have a business banking section where you can set up and submit payroll remittances online, which is one of the simplest ways to file and pay the deductions at source. Once you have registered for the service, you would "add" the Federal DAS and Quebec (if applicable) DAS forms to the forms that are filed regularly. These are then to be completed based on your remittance frequency by entering the information for each field and replaces the paper form entirely. The remittance is then taken directly from the bank account. Note that the filing date will be one business day before the due date, since the banks take one business day to process the payment.

- ONLINE (using CRA *My Payment*): You may also complete the DAS (payroll remittance) form using My Payment where , similar to online banking, you would enter your account number, number of employees, and amount payable and then make payment using Interac, Visa, or Mastercard (debit only).

- MAIL: You can complete the form that you receive in the mail from CRA for monthly deductions at source and enclose a cheque with it. If you don't have the payroll form from CRA (which can happen in the first month after registration or if you misplace it), you can create a document that lists the payroll account number, number of employees, and the amount of the remittance and submit it. If paying by cheque, you should mail it a few days in advance to ensure it is received by the due date and thereby avoid penalties.

Other Options to Pay Deductions at Source

There are third party services which allow you to pay by credit card. Note that a fee is charged in addition to the amount due to CRA. If you outsource your payroll to a third-party service such as ADP or Wagepoint, they will take care of remittances on your behalf.

You can also make payment, along with a payment remittance from CRA, in person at a bank or the post office.

What Are the Penalties for Late Filing Payroll DAS?

It is very important to ensure that you pay your remittances on time. Failure to file the source deductions return and make payment will result penalties as follows:

- 3% if the amount is one to three days late;
- 5% if it is four or five days late;
- 7% if it is six or seven days late;
- 10% if it is more than seven days late or if no amount is remitted.

Interest will also be charged on late payments, and there are a variety of other penalties that may apply.

How Do You Pay Monthly Remittances (Deductions at Source) to Revenu Québec?

Amounts to be remitted to Revenu Québec include Quebec Pension Plan (QPP), Quebec Parental Insurance Plan (QPIP), Quebec Health Services Fund (QHSF), and Quebec Income Taxes. Quebec employers are also required to pay CNESST and CNT. Note that QPP and QPIP include an employer portion, while QHSF, CNESST, and CNT are all 100% payable by the employer. RQ will also advise you of whether your filing frequency is monthly or quarterly.

Below are remittance and payment options for RQ:

- ONLINE (using Business Banking): Most banks will allow you to set up the Quebec DAS forms and pay online through the business banking service.

- ONLINE (using RQ *clicSÉQUR My Business Account*): You can submit your DAS by going to your business account with RQ and completing the source deduction form by filling out the appropriate fields. Once complete, RQ will provide you with a "payment code". You can then go to your business banking account, add this payment type, and simply enter the code to make payment.

- MAIL: RQ will also send you a form for monthly deductions at source. This will need to be completed and a cheque enclosed with it for the amount payable. If you don't have the payroll form from RQ, you can create a document which lists the following fields and amounts owing for each:
  - Period to which payroll relates
  - income tax withheld
  - QPP (employee and employer)
  - QPIP(employee and employer)
  - QHSF (employer only)
  - CNESST (employer only)

  If paying by cheque, similar to CRA, you should mail it a few days in advance to ensure it is received by the due date and thereby avoid penalties.

Revenu Québec has a comprehensive guide on source deductions and contributions.

Once you decide to take on employees, there are certain steps to follow to ensure that you are paying your employees and the revenue agencies correctly. Although these are a bit time consuming to set up, once you have established a routine, they are fairly easy to follow.

WHY YOU SHOULD REGISTER FOR CRA AND RQ *MY BUSINESS ACCOUNT* (AND HOW TO DO IT)

With all the data moving to the cloud these days and ubiquitous online access to banking, customer, and supplier portals, it makes sense that Revenue Canada (CRA) and Revenu Québec (RQ) have followed suit. Considerable resources have been spent by the revenue agencies on developing their online portals and encouraging both individual taxpayers and businesses to move the majority of their tax-related interactions online. (Almost every accountant conference has an appearance by a CRA representative talking about the improvements to their online portal and imploring accountants to convince their clients to make the switch). The upfront investment has resulted in significant cost savings for CRA/RQ (postage costs alone have dropped dramatically) while improving accuracy and perhaps most importantly (for the government) increasing the effectiveness of tax collection efforts. CRA personnel have been able to move away from verifying calculations and manually reviewing tax returns to more value-added analysis, which has allowed them to identify tax miscreants with higher accuracy.

Benefits of Registering for My Business Account with CRA and RQ

For both the individual taxpayer and small business owner, there are numerous benefits to registering.

1. ***My Business Account*** for both CRA and RQ gives you access to your payroll deductions at source paid, T4 summaries and slips, HST/GST and QST returns filed, payments made, instalments and corporate tax files including amounts paid to date , instalments, non-resident accounts and much more.

2. Ability to review all tax documents, including Notices of Assessment, in one place rather than having to save/scan them and inevitably lose them when needed most.

3. Being able to keep on top of tax obligations to avoid penalties, reduce interest charges, and running afoul of requests for information/audits due to missed or overlooked mail.

4. Submit documents relating to open queries/cases/authorizations online rather than faxing them in. (For some reason, fax is the only other non-mail way to send documents to CRA, which does not have access to email. They are among the last organizations to use fax technology. RQ is a little more advanced and has a secure server by which documents can be emailed; however, this usually has to be arranged with an individual representative.)

5. Consult statements of account to reconcile payments made to the various tax accounts. Often HST/GST and QST refunds, instead of being paid out to the business, will get allocated to corporate or payroll taxes payable (or vice versa). Being able to review the statement can greatly facilitate the reconciliation process.

6. Consult year-end tax balances e.g. capital and non-capital loss carry forwards, refundable dividend tax on

hand (RDTOH), and Capital dividend account balances (once they are verified) are all available on the CRA site.

7. You can add your accountant as an authorized user using CRA **Represent a Client** allowing them to retrieve Notices of Assessments directly or reconcile accounts to payments made.

8. GST and QST returns can be filed online using the Revenu Québec portal. Once filed, a payment code is generated that simplifies the payment of tax through online banking (by going to bank's tax payment and filing service and adding the payment type "Revenu Québec download code". To make payment, copy and paste the code and it will be allocated to the correct tax accounts).

   HST/GST returns can also be filed using CRA my business account. This is especially useful when the business is expecting a refund.

9. Year-end salary declarations including T4 and RL1 slips and RL1 summaries can be filed online rather than having to complete these by hand, mail them in, and hope that they arrive on time.

10. RQ provides you with a payment code for any tax obligations that are due including GST and QST and corporate taxes amounts owing and instalments. These can be retrieved from the business account. It is important to note that there are several different types of logins for Revenu Québec businesses, which can be confusing. It's a good idea to keep these recorded. When accessing the tax files, it is important to use the *My Business Account* link.

11. Once you have registered your business in Quebec, you can access the Registraire des Entreprises using the *clicSÉQUR* login and password at the *clicSÉQUR Entreprises* link to access details about your account, change addresses, and update your Annual Declaration.

How to Register for My Business Account

Online registration is also fairly straightforward. With CRA, identity verification can be provided by a banking partner, which can be seen on the registration page. You want to make sure that you have your Notices of Assessment (CRA or RQ, depending on which agency you are registering with) handy, and then follow the instructions to register. CRA will usually send a security code either in the mail or it can also be retrieved by calling them. Revenu Québec will generally want to call you to verify your identity.

1. CRA *My Business Account*

   Click on the *Register* button most appropriate to your situation.

2. RQ *My Business Account*

   Click on *Access My Account* and then follow the instructions for registration. You will be provided with a user name and password.

> ➤ *Make sure you save the user name and password; otherwise, you will have to call RQ later!*

Registration itself may take some time; however, once completed, it provides much more control over your tax situation, which can be the cause of a significant amount of stress for many business owners and their accountants.

HOW DO I PAY MY INCOME TAX AT THE END OF THE YEAR?

While being self-employed comes with numerous benefits, there are also many challenges. One of them is ensuring that you are aware of, and fulfill, your tax obligations on a timely basis. This helps to reduce stress as tax deadlines approach and can potentially result in significant tax savings as you keep track of all your tax deductions and avoid interest and penalties.

What Is a T2125?

If you are an unincorporated business owner, you are required to report the income from your business activities and are entitled to claim business-related expenses against the income of your business. The income and expenses are reported on a Business Declaration form, which is part of the regular personal tax return or T1 (TP1 in Quebec). This form is referred to as the *T2125 - Statement of Business and Professional Activities*.

What Types of Businesses Are Required to Prepare a T2125?

Basically, any type of activity that produces income (money that you "earn"), requires the inclusion of the T2125 as part of your personal tax return, as long as your business is not incorporated (corporations have different tax filing rules).

Broadly, this includes:

- Freelancers
- Independent Contractors
- Self-Employed Workers
- Sole Proprietorships
- Informal Employment
- Part-Time Income from a Hobby

While many of these terms are interchangeable, it is important to note that if you receive income on which no tax was paid, you should determine if it requires inclusion in a T2125 . Some more specific examples of this include:

- Selling goods, for a profit, on ebay or Etsy in your spare time
- Selling your services on Fiverr, Upwork, Freelancer, or any other similar type of service
- Earning ad revenues from your blog or YouTube Channel
- Driving for Uber or Lyft
- Selling online courses
- Donations to your website
- Payments for musical performances

What Kind of Documentation Do You Need?

Essentially, businesses are required to maintain proof of their business-related income and expenses. You are not required to enclose this with your tax return, but you will be asked for these documents in the event of an audit.

Income

The types of documentation for income include invoices to clients/customers for services and/or goods sold OR a statement from your customer (person or business) to whom you are providing the service. For example, while you don't invoice Google for ads, you can download a monthly statement reflecting the amount of ad revenues that have been paid along with your bank statement showing the amount received. Uber provides a tax summary at the end of the year as well as weekly breakdowns of earnings, which should be reconciled to the amount received in your bank account. It should be noted that revenues are required to be shown in the month that you earn them rather than when you receive payment; this is referred to as the accrual method. If you have invoiced someone in December, but were only paid in January, this amount would be considered to be income in December.

Expenses

For expenses, most importantly you will need to retain the receipt or bill from the supplier, along with the charge on your bank statement or credit card. If you are using subcontractors or casual labour, it is very important to have them send you a bill as this will be required as proof that the expense was incurred. If a bill is not available, other documentation such as an email confirmation indicating the amount and date paid might be sufficient. It is good practice to detail the business purpose on the bill or receipt, particularly for items that might be considered to be personal expenses, such as meals or travel expenses.

What Type of Information Do You Need to Complete the T2125?

Your accounting system, whether it is a spreadsheet or dedicated software, should be able to compile your information into a **profit-loss statement** that reflects total sales/revenues and lists the business expenses by category. A **pivot table** or **sub-totals by category** can be used on a spreadsheet, while any accounting software will provide a profit-loss statement.

To see what the breakdown by category looks like, please refer to the actual T2125 form available at CRA.

How to Prepare the T2125

Preparing the T2125 is fairly straightforward particularly when you use software. There are several software programs that can be used, including TurboTax, Ufile, Simple Tax, etc. Since these are all free to try (fees are applied once you have to print or file the return), it might be worth testing them out to see which one you are most comfortable with. I strongly encourage everyone to use software to prepare the return as, in addition to reducing completely avoidable errors such as calculation mistakes, they can help you maximize your deductions and optimize your taxes. Also, they allow you to electronically file the tax returns, which is a huge time saver and provides you with a confirmation that the taxes have been filed.

Most software will take you through an interview process where you confirm that you have a small business (or self-employed income). It should then open up the T2125 where you are required to enter details about your business, including the name, address, and type of service

or product that you provide (you can list more than one).
The software will also ask you to enter your NAICs code,
which corresponds to the type of business that you have.
Not all business fall neatly into a NAICs code, in which case
you should choose the one that you believe is most
appropriate.

> ➤ Note: Doing an internet search for your type of
> business + NAICs can provide some guidance on which
> code to use.

Once you have completed the basic information, you will
need to enter the income and expense amounts. If you
have prepared your income (profit-loss) statement as
mentioned above, this will be very straightforward as you
just enter the amounts per category. If an expense does
not fit any available category, you can enter it manually
under **Other Expenses**.

When entering income, it is important to note sales should
be entered net of HST/GST and QST charged (sales amount
before adding taxes). Any business-related income that
has been reported on a T4A should be entered in the
correct line corresponding to the box on the T4A (this is
usually box 28 or box 40).

There are three additional sections that must be
completed, if applicable:

1. Car Expenses:
   - For a vehicle used for a mix of personal and business,
     KMs driven during the year for which you have an
     automobile/mileage log indicating the business
     purposes of trips

- For a vehicle exclusively used for business, total KMs driven based on odometer readings at January 1st and December 31st

- Gas, repairs, insurance, registration, parking etc. expenses for the year

- Make and model of vehicles

- Purchase amount, date OR lease amounts, dates and term of lease

2. Home Office Expenses

Home office expenses are calculated based on the square footage of space in the home used exclusively as an office (note that in most situations you are only allowed one office) as a portion of the total square footage of your home in order to determine the percentage of personal vs business use. This percentage is applied to the following in order to calculate your deductible amounts:

- Mortgage Interest OR Rent

- Utilities

- Property Taxes

- Insurance

- Telephone/Internet

- Whole-home expenses (e.g. alarm)

3. Capital Expenditures to Calculate CCA:

This represents purchases for a business that have a useful life exceeding 1 year and cost at least a few hundred dollars. For example, a computer, furniture, equipment etc. would all considered to be capital costs and are depreciated over time rather than expensed in one year. These expenses should be removed from your profit-loss statement and entered on the CCA schedule by selecting the correct CCA Class. For example, a computer would be Class 50, while furniture is Class 8.

Once all the data has been entered, the tax software will take care of the calculations. Many business owners ask me if they can prepare their own T2125 as part of their personal tax return, and I often encourage them to do so. As long as you are organized with your financial information and are able to work through some of the minor complexities without too much frustration, then it doesn't have to be painful (particularly after you have done it the first time). However, if you find that you are struggling with the terminology, or numbers just aren't your thing, then it might be better and less costly to hire an accountant.

APPENDIX A: REGISTER OR INCORPORATE YOUR BUSINESS

Business Structures

When embarking on a new business venture, one of the first decisions that has to be made is the type of legal structure that best suits the needs of the new business. In Canada, there are essentially two choices:

- **Business Registration** (Sole Proprietorship, Partnership)

  Registered businesses are simply an extension of the individual and as such the regulatory and tax obligations are relatively minimal. Setting up a small business is a fairly simple and inexpensive process. The owner is responsible for the debts of the business and pays taxes (or can deduct losses) on their personal tax return.

- **Incorporation**

  A corporation is a legal entity whose shareholders are separate from the business. Setting up a corporation is more complex than a business registration. Decisions have to be made regarding the jurisdiction the corporation will be established in (Federal vs Provincial), who will serve as directors, what shareholders will own the corporation, what the share structure will be, and how the owner and/or officers will be remunerated. The corporation assumes the debt obligations and pays taxes at a corporate level. Finally, a corporation, being a separate "person", enjoys limited liability, which is defined by Revenue Canada as follows:

As a general rule, the shareholders of a corporation are not responsible for its debts. If the corporation goes bankrupt, a shareholder will not lose more than his or her investment (unless the shareholder has provided personal guarantees for the corporation's debts). Creditors also cannot sue shareholders for liabilities (debts) incurred by the corporation, even though shareholders are owners of the corporation. Note, however, that if a shareholder has another relationship with the corporation — for example, as a director — then he or she may, in certain circumstances, be liable for the debts of the corporation.

Which Structure Is Best?

Like many small business decisions, whether to register or incorporate depends on the business owner's specific set of circumstances. When deciding on which structure to use, there are several questions that a small business owner should consider:

1. Does the new business venture need limited liability? Or will insurance be an adequate replacement?

A corporation creates a new legal entity that is distinct from the creator. As such, the liability of the company is limited to the shareholders' investment. (This does not apply in the case of personal guarantees or where directors have specific obligations etc.) This means that, in most cases, if a corporation is sued, its potential losses are limited to the assets of the corporation. Note that there are some cases where director's liability applies or where the corporate owner(s) is personally liable for the debts of a corporation.

2.   **As the owner/shareholder of the corporation, are you able to leave funds in the business or will you need to withdraw all of the profits of the business for living expenses?**

If the profit/cash flow of the corporation exceeds the amount required by the owner for salaries and expenses, the excess amounts can be left in the corporation. There are several strategies for corporate small business investments; many financial institutions tailor investment products specifically for corporations. It should be noted that passive income (investment, rental etc.) are taxed at a higher rate than business income; the rate is approximately 50% in most provinces. This is accumulated in the corporation as a refundable dividend tax that is refunded to the shareholder upon payment of dividends.

3.   **Are you willing and able to spend additional fees on incorporation costs and ongoing maintenance costs?**

There are costs relating to setting up a corporation and ongoing maintenance, including governmental, legal, and accounting fees that are usually higher than for a sole proprietorship.

4.   **Are you comfortable with the increased reporting requirements for a corporation, as you will mostly likely require the services of an accountant and possibly a lawyer?**

A separate set of legal and accounting records needs to be maintained. The accounting function is more involved since the reporting required for the corporate tax return is more extensive and often requires actual accounting software rather than just an spreadsheet, which is what many unincorporated business owners use. Additionally, a corporation needs to file an Annual Return and a corporate Tax Return each year that is separate from each shareholder's personal Tax Return. Any changes to the corporation's structure, address, etc. must be registered.

5. Do your clients, bank, or other stakeholders require that you incorporate, or do you need the credibility associated with having a corporation?

Certain business relationships may require the intermediary structure of a corporation, and "Inc.", "Limited", and "Corporation" all carry a certain social cachet.

6. Do you have plans to build an enduring business which you might want to transfer upon your retirement or death?

Because a sole-proprietorship essentially IS the owner, the actual business ceases operations when the owner does (though assets may be sold/transferred). In contrast, a corporation can continue long after the original shareholders have sold or bequeathed their shares.

> ➤ *Note: Owners of small business shares benefit from a lifetime capital gains exemption of $866,912. This allows a shareholder to sell the shares of qualifying corporations tax-free for gains up to $866,000 Note that this represents the full amount of the gain. The actual taxable capital gains is 50% of this amount: $433,456. The balance of $433,000 is non-taxable in the hands of the shareholder.*

Other Factors to Consider:

1. **Lower Tax Rates:** Corporations, particularly small businesses, benefit from corporate tax rates that are lower than individual tax rates. The combined Federal and

Provincial corporate tax rate in Quebec is 26.6%, while the small business corporate rate in Quebec ranges between 15% and 20.6%, depending of the number of hours worked by employees in the corporation. Note that lower tax rates do not usually apply to incorporated rental properties and other types of investment-related businesses that generate passive income, unless you have 6 or more employees.

2.   **Jurisdiction:** If you do decide to incorporate, you will have to decide whether a Federal or Provincial corporation is more appropriate. A Federal corporation is more expensive; however, it provides heightened name protection and additional credibility and might make more sense if you are planning to operate your business in the rest of Canada and/or internationally.

3.   **Owner Remuneration:** Owner-managed corporations need to determine the method and amount of remuneration. While registered business owners are simply taxed on the profits of the business, a corporation must pay salaries or dividends to its owners as employees or shareholders respectively. Note that there are no restrictions on having employees whether you are registered or incorporated.

4.   **Access to Capital:** Corporations generally have more ways of raising capital e.g. they can issue shares or sell bonds. Banks are often more comfortable lending to corporate entities with some established history. A corporation can be perceived as more professional than a sole proprietorship.

5.   **Income Splitting:** Shares of corporations can be allocated among family members, allowing them to draw dividend income from the business. Keep in mind that the

federal government targeted this type of tax planning and has imposed a set of criteria that evaluates the tax rate on dividends received by family members of business owners (Note: this does not apply to salaries). Although the rules are very complex, the new TOSI (tax on split income) legislation essentially attempts to determine whether the shareholder is actively involved in the corporation, specifically younger shareholders, to ensure that owners are not trying to reduce their tax bills by allocating dividends to related taxpayers with much lower personal tax rates.

6.   **Complex Structure and Taxation:** Corporations by their nature are more complex. Additionally, there are numerous tax considerations that can arise from corporate transactions including use of assets for personal reasons, transfer of assets to related parties, tax on capital, dividends to related family members (see above), etc.

7.   **Losses:** Corporate losses remain within the corporation and cannot be transferred to the shareholder, whereas, with a sole proprietorship, losses, with certain exceptions, can be offset against other sources of income thereby reducing taxes payable. A corporation may however amalgamate with another corporation to utilize its losses.

If you feel that your business is still in its infancy and there are no issues relating to liability or external requirements to incorporate, it might make sense to wait and see how the business evolves. A registered small business can decide to incorporate at any time, although if you do decide to take the next step and incorporate, there may be issues relating to "rollover" of assets and liabilities to a new entity that should be discussed with a lawyer or accountant.

APPENDIX B: HOW TO REGISTER A SMALL BUSINESS IN QUEBEC

If you have decided to simply register your business rather than incorporate and you are located in Quebec, the process is actually quite straightforward. Below we look at the questions that you need answer to determine your business registration obligations in Quebec.

What Types of Businesses Are Required to Register?

If you want to start an unincorporated business, whereby you **ONLY use your own first and last name** to invoice and transact with your customers, then technically no registration is required. This is can apply to a diverse range of business owners/self-employed individuals including artists, writers, and eBay sellers, who do not necessarily need a business name.

If you decide that you want to have a business name that is even slightly different from your given first and last name, then you are required to register your business. For example, many business owners use a different name for their websites or even an informal name that is used to communicate with customers.

Anyone who plans to start a tobacco retail outlet or a tanning salon must register with the Registraire des Entreprises (Enterprise Register), even if they only use their given first and last names.

How to Register Your Sole Proprietorship

The registration process is explained at the Quebec Enterprise Register, which is also where the registration process is initiated.

The registration for Sole Proprietorships can be found online at this link. The service is only available in French; however, using a translate function (such as Google Translate) can make this easier if you have difficulty navigating it in French. Using this link you can either register for the first time or re-register a business if you are changing the name of the business.

The registration declaration must be sent to the Registraire des Entreprises no later than 60 days after the date on which registration is required, except for business who have started a tobacco retail outlet or an artificial tanning salon, in which case he or she must file the declaration within 30 days of the start of the operation.

The fees to register a business with the Registraire des Entreprises are quite reasonable at $36 for a sole proprietorship and $53 for a partnership. There is also a priority service for which the fees are a little higher. The annual renewal fee for a sole proprietorship in Quebec is also $36. For the full list of fees, you can consult the fees and terms of payment document from Revenu Québec.

To file a registration declaration, you will have to provide the following information, depending on the situation:

1. the name and address of the signatory of the request;
2. the name of the natural person;

3. any other name that the natural person uses and under which he identifies himself in the exercise of his activities in Québec, if applicable;
4. the home address of the natural person;
5. the address of the elected domicile as well as the name of the person authorized to receive the documents of the natural person;
6. the two main activities of the enterprise;
7. the number of employees whose place of work is located in Québec;
8. the name and address of establishments located in Québec and the activities carried on there;
9. if applicable, the name and address of the administrator of the property of others, his function and the duration of his mandate;
10. if applicable, the name and address of the authorized representative;
11. the contact details of the person to contact in case the Registraire des Entreprises needs additional information to process the request.

The name of the business that you wish to register must conform with the following requirements:

- to Article 17 of the Corporate Legal Publicity Act
- to section I of the Regulation respecting the application of the Act respecting the legal publicity of sole proprietorships, partnerships, and legal persons
- to the Regulation respecting the language of commerce and business (this means that you must provide a French name that is equivalent to your English name, if applicable)

You can contact the Registraire des Enterprises by either sending an email or phoning them.

Once you have completed the form, RDE will review your application including the suitability of the name that you have chosen for your business. If you they accept your application, they will provide you with a Numero d'Entreprise Quebec (NEQ) which is the official number of your business (and can be used to establish that you are a registered business, set up bank accounts etc.). If they reject your application, they will let you know by mail, and you will have to start again at the beginning of the process.

How to Register Your Partnership or Corporation

If you are setting up a general or limited liability partnership or a corporation that has an office Quebec, then you must also register at the Quebec Enterprise Register. The following Registration procedures page provides you with links to the forms that are available online based on the type of business structure that you select. Alternatively, you can ask that the forms be mailed to you by contacting Revenu Québec or you can go in person to one of their offices. (They can be found at Complexe Desjardins in Montreal.)

Other Considerations

- Even if you are not required to register, Revenu Québec advises:

  "You can register voluntarily to make public the existence of your enterprise. You will then have the same rights and obligations as an enterprise that is legally bound to register."

- Regardless of whether you register, or how much revenue you generate, you are required to include all sales of goods and services, both on your Federal and Quebec tax return, and reflect it as business income on the T2125. Any expenses incurred to generate business income are then deductible.

- Once registered you are required to submit an Annual Declaration updating your registration along with the annual fee. This can be done through your personal tax return.

As long as you are aware of your obligations, registering a business in Quebec is a fairly straightforward process and much of it can be accomplished somewhat painlessly online. Once set up, it is important to ensure that you maintain adequate records of revenues and expenses and file the necessary government returns thus ensuring that you can attend to the business of running your business.

APPENDIX C: HOW TO PAY GST/QST USING ONLINE BANKING

How to Sign-Up for Business Tax Payments

All businesses, including sole proprietorships, partnerships, and corporations that have a separate business bank account with a CRA-approved bank, can make payments through the government tax payment and filing service. Signing up for this service can usually be done online: When you log-in to your business portal, the service can usually be found in the **Bill Payments/ Pay Bills** section. Once you have agreed to the terms and completed the registration, you are ready to pay businesses taxes online. Each type of payment is represented by a different form that has to be "added" before payment can be made.

HST/GST and QST Payments and Instalments

In order to file and pay the federal HST/GST payment, the first step is to add the relevant payment type. The HST/GST number can be found on any of the GST forms received or through CRA My Business Account. Similarly, the QST number can be found through correspondence or RQ **clicSÉQUR My Business Account**. The HST/GST and QST numbers only needs to be added one time.

Below are a list of forms and description:

Federal Forms

HST/GST Return and Payment -- GST34 -- (GST34)

When you want to complete the entire HST/GST return online, this is the form to select. You are required to enter the period to which the return applies, whether quarterly, monthly, or annual. The due date is the date the return is due. Note that the filing should always be done at least one day prior to the due date as it takes one day to process. The due date reflected on the return can also be an earlier date (this will not make a difference to the due date that CRA or RQ have on file).

- Line 101 is total sales for the period being reported on.
- Line 105 is the HST/GST tax collected on the sales from line 101.
- Line 108 is the HST/GST tax paid on purchases.
- Line 110 allows you to enter instalments paid, if any during the year.

HST/GST Balance Due -- GST-B -- (RC177).

This is the form to use when you have received a Notice of Assessment for HST/GST and need to pay the amount due. This can be for interest and penalties or relate to a form that was filed but payment has not yet been made.

HST/GST Payment Only -- GST-P -- (GST-P)

This form can be used to make instalments for those who have annual filing periods, but whose HST/GST exceeds $3,000 and are therefore required to make quarterly instalments.

Quebec Forms

For those businesses that are registered in Quebec, both GST and QST are administered by Revenu Québec. Only one "Combined" form is required to pay both taxes.

Combined HST/GST + QST Remittance -- G-QST -- (FPZ-500.IF)

This is similar to the "Federal - HST/GST Return and Payment -- GST34" explained above. The information required is the same plus the same line numbers for Quebec including 205, which is QST Collected and 208 which is QST Paid on Expenses.

Combined GST + QST Instalment -- TXIN -- (FPZ-558)

This form, similar to the Federal payment only form above, can be used to make instalments for those who have annual filing periods but their HST/GST and QST each (individually) exceed $3,000 and are therefore required to make quarterly instalments.

APPENDIX D: SALES TAX IN OTHER PROVINCES

While many Canadian provinces have harmonized their sales tax with the Federal government by charging HST, there are some provinces that have a distinct sales tax regime.

Below is a table of sales tax rates by province:

Province	Type	GST	HST	PST	Total Rate
Alberta	GST	5%			5%
British Columbia	GST + PST	5%		7%	12%
Manitoba	GST + PST	5%		7%	12%
New Brunswick	HST		15%		15%
Newfoundland & Labrador	HST		15%		15%
Northwest Territories	GST	5%			5%
Nova Scotia	HST		15%		15%
Nunavut	GST	5%			5%
Ontario	HST		13%		13%
Prince Edward Island	HST		15%		15%
Quebec	GST + QST	5%		9.975%	14.975%
Saskatchewan	GST + PST	5%		6%	11%
Yukon	GST	5%			5%

There are 4 provinces in which there is a distinct sales tax rate, that is not part of GST/HST and for which you need to register separately and file returns. These provinces are British Columbia, Manitoba, Saskatchewan. and Quebec.

British Columbia (B.C.) Provincial Sales Tax (PST)

The B.C. provincial sales tax (PST) is a retail sales tax that applies when a taxable good or service is purchased, acquired, or brought into B.C. for use in B.C., unless a specific exemption applies.

The B.C. sales tax rate of 7% applies to the following categories:

- The purchase or lease of new and used goods in B.C.
- Goods brought, sent, or delivered into B.C. for use in B.C.
- The purchase of:
  - Software
  - Services to goods such as vehicle maintenance, furniture assembly, computer repair
  - Accommodation
  - Legal services
  - Telecommunication services, including internet services and digital and electronic media content, such as music and movies
  - Gifts of vehicles, boats, and aircraft

There are also a number of exceptions for goods and services on which PST is not required to be collected, including the following:

- Food for human consumption (e.g. basic groceries and prepared food such as restaurant meals)
- Books, newspapers, and magazines
- Children-sized clothing
- Bicycles
- Prescription medications and household medical aids such as cough syrup and pain medications

The chart below shows the reporting periods which is dependent on how much sales tax you collect:

PST collectable per year	Ongoing reporting period
$3,000 or less	Quarterly, semi-annual or annua
More than $3,000 up to $6,000	Quarterly or semi-annual
More than $6,000 up to $12,000	Monthly or quarterly
More than $12,000	Monthly only

For more details relating to B.C. PST, please refer to the guidance on the government of BC website.

Note: As of April 1st, 2021, B.C. started requiring businesses that are not resident in B.C. but sell goods and services on which the PST is applicable to B.C. residents to register for PST. Full details on this can be found here.

Manitoba Provincial Retail Sales Tax (RST)

The Retail Sales Tax (RST) is a tax applied to the retail sale or rental of most goods and certain services in Manitoba. The tax is calculated on the selling price, before the GST (Good and Services Tax) is applied.

The provincial sales tax rate is 7%.

Your business is required to be registered for sales tax if:

you carry on business in Manitoba, selling taxable goods or services at retail

you are a manufacturer, wholesaler, or importer in Manitoba (directly or through an agent)

you bring into or receive in Manitoba, taxable goods for use by your business

you are an out-of-province business that solicits and sells goods in Manitoba

you are a mechanical or electrical (M&E) contractor performing work in Manitoba

you operate a retail business in Manitoba on a temporary, short-term or intermittent basis

You are not required to be registered for Manitoba sales tax if:

your business sells only non-taxable goods or services

you are a contractor (except an M&E contractor) who only supplies and installs goods into real property and you buy all goods from sellers registered for Manitoba retail sales tax

your business's annual taxable sales volume is under $10,000, and you buy all goods from sellers registered for Manitoba retail sales tax

For more details relating to Manitoba PST, please refer to this pamphlet issued by the government of Manitoba.

Saskatchewan Provincial Sales Tax (PST)

The Saskatchewan sales tax applies to taxable goods and services consumed or used in Saskatchewan. It applies to goods and services purchased in the province as well as goods and services imported for consumption or use in Saskatchewan. Both new and used goods are subject to tax.

The Saskatchewan sales tax rate of 6% applies to the following categories:

- accounting and bookkeeping services
- advertising services
- architectural services
- commercial building cleaning services
- computer services
- credit reporting or collection services
- dry cleaning and laundry services
- employment placement services
- engineering services
- extended warranty and maintenance contracts
- legal services
- lodging services
- real estate services
- repair or installation services related to tangible personal property
- security and investigation services
- telecommunication services
- telephone answering services
- veterinary services
- services to real property

Certain goods are exempt from PST in Saskatchewan, including:

- basic groceries
- reading materials
- agricultural equipment
- prescription drugs and medicine

For more details relating to Saskatchewan PST, please refer to this information bulletin issued by the government of Saskatchewan.

START YOUR BUSINESS CHECKLIST

1. Decide on a name for your business.	
2. Register your business in the province in which you and your business are located.	
3. Set up a separate business bank account and credit card.	
4. Determine if you need to register for sales tax.	
5. Evaluate if the Quick Method of calculating sales tax is more beneficial.	
6. Register for HST/GST with CRA* or if in Quebec, HST/GST and QST with RQ**, if required.	
7. Register for a payroll number with CRA and if located in Quebec RQ, if you plan to hire employees.	
8. Register for CRA My Business Account or RQ My Business Account, if located in Quebec.	
9. Evaluate what type of accounting system you are going to use e.g. spreadsheet, accounting software, or outsource.	
10. Decide how you plan to do your income taxes – DIY using software or outsource.	

ABOUT THE AUTHOR

My name is Ronika Khanna. I am a Chartered Professional Accountant (CPA), Chartered Accountant (CA), and Chartered Financial Analyst (CFA), and the founder of Montreal Financial, an accounting, tax, and financial consulting services business. After having worked as an accounting professional for several companies, both in Canada and Bermuda, including with Pricewaterhouse Coopers (PwC) and ING Risk Management Limited, I decided to launch my own business, focusing primarily on the accounting, tax, and financial needs of small business owners, start-ups, and independent contractors.

I have helped numerous small businesses with their financial, accounting, and tax reporting over the years, which has allowed them to run their businesses more effectively and profitably. I wrote this book to make starting a small business as easy as possible.

You can connect with me by visiting my website at https://www.montrealfinancial.ca. You can also subscribe to my biweekly newsletter where I discuss topics of interest to small businesses.

OTHER BOOKS BY RONIKA KHANNA

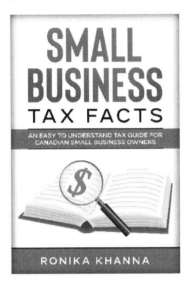

Starting a business or becoming self-employed opens up a whole new world of tax considerations. This book will guide you through the fundamentals to ensure that you pay the taxes you need to but no more than that. In learning about the different types of tax and the sorts of deductions that businesses are entitled to you can have a better understanding of your small business tax and save time and money.

For small business owners, administrators, and bookkeepers, this book will help you to understand everything you need to know about paying yourself using small business dividends. Step by step instructions guide you through preparing and submitting your own tax filings to the government.

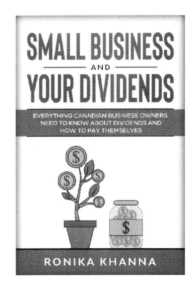

EXCERPT FROM "SMALL BUSINESS TAX FACTS": UNDERSTANDING INCOME AND TAX

Income tax in Canada was presented as a temporary measure to help finance the significant costs of World War I. It was introduced in 1916 on business profits and extended in 1917 to all individuals whose income exceeded a certain amount. Prior to the introduction of income tax, government revenues came from duties, excise taxes, and revenues from the postal service. Although income tax remained in place, it wasn't actually made permanent until 1949.

Income tax has become significantly more complex since its introduction over 100 years ago. The original tax act was only 10 pages long, while it now stands at over 3,500 pages. The income tax act is a weighty tome that takes many years of education and practice to understand and parts of it are still incomprehensible to many accountants and tax professionals (and Revenue Canada agents). So, while it would seem challenging for the average layperson to try and understand, the fundamentals of tax as they apply to most individuals and small business owners are actually pretty straightforward. Whether or not you do your own tax return, it is my belief that all Canadians should be familiar with the basic concepts of tax as an essential component of understanding their financial situation. As an accountant for many years, I have encountered much anxiety around the topic of tax. I have written this book in an attempt to explain some of the fundamental concepts of tax as they apply to individuals and small business owners.

What Is Income Tax?

Income tax, very simply, is a tax imposed by the government that is based on an individual or business's income. The purpose of income tax is to generate revenues to fund numerous services and projects, from healthcare to building roads. The complexity arises in how the amount of that income is determined and what type of tax rates apply. Different sources of income are treated differently for tax purposes, while different levels of income have different tax rates. Canada has a progressive tax system, which means that not every dollar of income earned is treated equally. Rather, taxation rates gradually increase as your income increases, which means that those who earn more not only pay a greater **amount** of tax in number of dollars, but they also pay a higher **rate** of tax in percentage of income. For example, all things being equal, someone earning $100,000 will pay more than double the amount of tax that someone earning $50,000 pays.

Tax Brackets, Average Tax Rates, and Marginal Tax Rates

In order to understand the progressive tax system, you need to first understand the concepts of a) tax brackets, b) average tax rate, and c) marginal tax rate.

Tax brackets are a set of ranges that indicate the amount of tax you will pay on income earned within that range. An analogy would be a series of buckets. Your income fills the first tax bracket up to a specified amount. Any income earned in addition to the first tax bracket is then put into the second tax bracket, which is also capped at a specified amount. This goes on until either your income has been fully allocated or you reach the top tax bracket, which has no upper limit.

❖ **Example**:

Donna earns a salary $100,000 as a web developer for the Canada Computer Company. She lives in Ontario and is single. She has no other sources of income.

If Donna lived in a country which used a flat tax system with a rate of 20%, she would simply pay tax of $20,000 and be done with it.

In Canada, which uses a progressive tax system, Donna's income of $100,000 falls into several tax brackets as follows:

2020 Tax Rate	2020 Tax Brackets	Donna's Salary	Tax
15.00%	48,535.00	48,535.00	7,280.25
20.50%	97,069.00	48,534.00	9,949.47
26.00%	150,473.00	2,931.00	762.06
33.00%	214,368.00		
	Total Earnings	**100,000.00**	**17,991.78**
	Average Tax Rate		**17.99%**
	Marginal Tax Rate		**26.00%**

❖ Of the $100,000 of income that Donna has received in 2020, $48,535 fills up the first bucket for which she is taxed at a rate of 15% for $7,280.25.

The next bucket fills up with $48,534 of income which is taxed at 20.50% for $9,949.47.

The remaining amount of $2,931 exceeds the second tax bracket and is then put into the third bucket. Only the amount of $2,931 is taxed 26% for $762.06.

We can also calculate the **average tax rate**. By totaling the amounts that Donna pays per tax bracket, we see that she pays $17.991.78 in income tax. Donna's average tax rate is derived by taking the total taxes payable and dividing it by her income. The **average tax rate** is the effective rate at which Donna is taxed. It is <u>not</u> the average of the tax rates per bracket.

The final concept is the **marginal tax rate,** which is the amount of additional tax paid for every additional dollar earned as income. It is important to note there that her entire income is not taxed at the top tax bracket or the marginal tax rate. Only the portion that exceeds the previous tax brackets, which is $2,931 in this case, is taxed at 26%. The **marginal tax rate** is the top rate that Donna pays, but it is <u>not</u> the actual rate her whole income is taxed at.

> ➤ Note: Our example above only shows federal tax. Each province also imposes a provincial tax with different tax brackets which is then added on to the tax liability above. There is also a basic tax credit which in 2020 exempts the first $12,298 of income from tax. Tax credits are explained further below.

Manufactured by Amazon.ca
Bolton, ON

27811253R00068